"For God's Words are life, they are healing and health to **my** entire body.

- Proverbs 4:22

PERSONALIZED

healing

SCRIPTURES

MyVersion LLC.

Personalized Healing Scriptures
Print Edition
ISBN 13: 979-8-89846-004-4
Copyright © 2025 MyVersion LLC.

Published by MyVersion LLC.
https://MyVersionBook.com

Contents

Introduction ---------------------- i

Personal Promises from the
Old Covenant ------------- 1

Personal Realities in the
New Covenant ------ 17

Prayer for Healing ------------- 41

Prayer for Salvation and Baptism
in the Holy Spirit -------------- 43

Introduction

The Healing Power of the Word

The Bible is clear that it's God's will for us all to be healed and to live in complete health and wholeness. God is not only able, but willing to heal you, deliver you, and prosper you in every area of life.

God has provided the way for you to be well—completely and totally well—because He is a good Father and does only good. God has nothing but great plans and an awesome future in store for you!

Our heavenly Father has an important work for each of us in the body of Christ to do. It will require a strong, healthy body with totally healed members. That's why we all need to walk in complete health.

Speaking His Word about our health is what keeps us healed! Proverbs 4:22 says that God's Words are healing and health to our bodies. That is powerful!

See, the key to staying healed and whole is speaking healing scriptures over yourself. This is not something mystical or magical. This is just how faith works. Romans 10:17 says that faith comes by hearing and hearing by the Word of God. When you hear yourself speaking the Word of God, faith rises up and accesses the healing that Jesus made available when he died on the cross for you.

This book is broken up into two sections, one containing the promises from the Old Covenant (Old Testament) and the other containing your realities in the New Covenant (New Testament). The entire Bible is inspired by God and is useful for teaching (2 Timothy 3:16) so as New Testament believers, we can stand on God's Word both in the Old and New Testament.

As you read through this book, take ownership of the Scriptures you read and speak them over yourself as reality in your life. Faith will rise up, and you will see big changes in your body and life.

Personal Promises from the Old Covenant

If **I** will diligently listen and obey the voice of the Lord **my** God and will do what is right in His sight, and will listen to and obey His commandments and keep all His statutes, God will not allow any of the diseases upon **me** which were brought upon the Egyptians, for God is the Lord Who heals **me**.

- Exodus 15:26

When **I** serve the Lord **my** God; the Lord blesses **my** food and water, and the Lord takes away all sickness from **my** body.

- Exodus 23:25

The Lord protects **me** from all sickness and disease, He doesn't let **me** suffer from all of the terrible diseases of Egypt.

- Deuteronomy 7:15

"If **I** will diligently listen to the voice of the Lord **my** God, being watchful and alert to do all the commandments which He commands **me** today, the Lord God will set **me** high above all the nations of the earth. And all these blessings shall come upon **me** and overtake **me** if **I** heed the voice of the Lord **my** God.

- Deuteronomy 28:1-2

The Lord calls heaven and earth to witness the choice that **I** will make today. The Lord has set before **me** life and death, blessings and curses; therefore **I** choose life, that **my** descendants and **I** may live and may love the Lord God, obey His voice, and cling to Him. For the Lord is **my** life and the length of **my** days, that **I** may dwell in the land which the Lord swore to give to **my** fathers, to Abraham, Isaac, and Jacob.

- Deuteronomy 30:19-20

Every single good and perfect promise that the LORD has given **me** has come true.

- Joshua 21:45

Praise the Lord who has given **me** rest, just as He promised. Not one word has failed of all the wonderful promises He has given to **me**, His servant.

- 1 Kings 8:56

The Lord will not break his covenant with **me**, nor will He alter the thing that is gone out of His lips.

- Psalm 89:34

With long life will the Lord satisfies **me** and shows **me** His salvation.

- Psalm 91:16

The Lord forgives all **my** iniquities, He heals each one of **my** diseases.

- Psalm 103:3

He brought them forth also with silver and gold: and there was not one feeble person among their tribes.

- Psalm 105:37

The Lord sent out His Word and healed **me**, snatching **me** from the door of death.

- Psalm 107:20

I will not die; instead, **I** will live to declare the works and recount the illustrious acts of the Lord.

- Psalm 118:17

I trust in the Lord with all **my** heart, and do not rely on **my** own understanding. In all **my** ways , **I** acknowledge Him, and the Lord makes **my** paths smooth.

- Proverbs 3:5-6

I pay attention to the Lord's words; **I** consent and submit to His sayings. **I** don't let them leave **my** sight; **I** let them penetrate deep into the center of **my** heart. For they are life to **me**, healing and health to **my** flesh. Also, **I** keep and guard **my** heart with all vigilance, for it determines the course of **my** life.

- Proverbs 4:20-23

I do not fear! [there is nothing to fear], for the Lord, is with **me**; **I** do not look around in terror and **I'm** not discouraged, for the Lord is **my** God. The Lord strengthens **me** and hardens **me** to difficulties, yes, the Lord helps **me**; yes, the Lord holds **me** up and retains **me** with His victorious right hand of right-eousness and justice. For the Lord God holds **my** right hand; The Lord says to **me**, "Fear not; I will help you!"

- *Isaiah* 41:10;13

Yes! The Lord is the one who blots out and cancels **my** transgressions, for His own sake, and He does not remember **my** sins. **I** put the Lord in remembrance [**I** remind Him of **my** merits]... The Lord sets forth **my** case that **I** may be justified (proved right).

- *Isaiah* 43:25-26

"The Lord has borne **my** weaknesses (sicknesses, griefs, and distresses) and carried **my** sorrows and pains, yet the world ignorantly considered Him stricken, smitten, and afflicted by God. But He was wounded for **my** transgressions, He was bruised for **my** guilt and iniquities; the chastisement needed to obtain peace and well-being was upon Him, and with the stripes [that wounded] Him, **I** am healed and made whole.

- *Isaiah* 53:4-5

Then the Lord said to **me**, "You have seen well, for I am alert and active, watching over My Word to perform it."

- Jeremiah 1:12

The Lord restores health to **me**, and heals **my** wounds, because they have called **me** an outcast...

- Jeremiah 30:17

I will beat plowshares into swords, and **my** pruning hooks into spears; **I** will say, "I am a strong warrior!"

- Joel 3:10

The Lord is so good, **my** strength and stronghold in the day of trouble; He knows, cares for, and understands **me**, when **I** takes refuge and trust in Him.

Whatever plot the enemy devises against **me**, the Lord will make a complete end of it; **my** affliction will not occur twice.

- Nahum 1:7-9

Personal Realities in the New Covenant

And behold, a leper approached Jesus and, laying on his face, worshiped Him, saying, Lord, if You are willing, You are able to cleanse me and make me whole. And Jesus reached out His hand and touched him, saying, I am willing; be cleansed and cured. And instantly his leprosy was cured and cleansed.

- Matthew 8:2-3

And Jesus fulfilled what was spoken by the prophet Isaiah, He Himself took [in order to carry away] all **my** weaknesses and infirmities and carried away all **my** diseases.

- Matthew 8:17

The Lord says, whatever **I** forbid and declare to be improper and unlawful on earth must be what is already forbidden in heaven, and whatever **I** permit and declare proper and lawful on earth must be what is already permitted in heaven. Again the Lord says, if **I** and another on earth agree (harmonize together, make a symphony together) about whatever [anything and everything] **we** may ask, it will come to pass and be done for **us** by My Father in heaven. For wherever two or three are gathered in My name, there the Lord [I AM] is in the midst of them.

- Matthew 18:18-20

...If **I** have faith and do not doubt, **I** will not only do what has been done to the fig tree, but even if **I** say to this mountain, Be taken up and cast into the sea, it will be done.

- *Matthew* 21:21

I will pick up serpents; and [even] if **I** drink anything deadly, it will not hurt **me**; **I** will lay **my** hands on the sick, and they will get well and recover.

- *Mark* 16:18

Behold! the Lord has given **me** authority and power to trample upon serpents and scorpions, and [physical and mental] strength and ability over all the power that the enemy [possesses]; and nothing shall in any way harm **me**.

– *Luke* 10:19

I know that God does not listen to sinners; but because **I** am God-fearing, a worshiper of Him, and **I** do His will, God listens to **me**.

– *John* 9:31

The thief comes only in order to steal and kill and destroy. Jesus came that **I** may have life, and have it in abundance (to the full, till it overflows).

– *John* 10:10

Abraham did not weaken in faith when he considered the impotence of his own body, which was as good as dead because he was about a hundred years old, or when he considered the barrenness of Sara's deadened womb. Just like Abraham, no unbelief or distrust makes **me** waver or doubtingly question concerning the promise of God, but **I** grow strong and am empowered by faith as **I** give praise and glory to God, Fully satisfied and assured that God is able and mighty to keep His Word and to do what He has promised.

- Romans 4:19-21

And if the Spirit of Him who raised up Jesus from the dead dwells in **me**, then He Who raised up Christ Jesus from the dead will also restore to life **my** mortal body through the Holy Spirit who dwells in **me**.

- *Romans* 8:11

For as many as are the promises of God to **me**, they all find their Yes [answer] in Christ. For this reason **I** also utter "Amen" (so be it) to God through Him to the glory of God.

- *1 Corinthians* 1:20

Christ purchased **my** freedom, redeeming **me** from the curse of the Law and its condemnation by Himself becoming a curse for **me**, for it is written, cursed is everyone who hangs on a tree (is crucified);

- Galatians 3:13

And **I** am convinced and sure of this very thing, that He Who began a good work in **me** will continue it until the return of Jesus Christ, developing that good work and perfecting and bringing it to full completion in **me**.

- Philippians 1:6

Not in **my** own strength for God is all the while effectually at work in **me** energizing and creating in **me** the power and desire, both to will and to do for His good pleasure, satisfaction and delight.

- *Philippians* 2:13

I do not fret or have any anxiety about anything, but in every circumstance and in everything, by prayer and petition (definite requests), with thanksgiving, **I** continue to make **my** wants known to God. And God's peace will be

mine, [that tranquil state of a soul assured of its salvation through Christ, and so fearing nothing from God and being content with its earthly lot of whatever sort that is, that peace] which transcends all understanding, garrisons and mount guard over **my** heart and mind in Christ Jesus. For the rest; whatever is true, whatever is worthy of reverence and is honorable and seemly, whatever is just, whatever is pure, whatever is lovely and lovable, whatever is kind and gracious, if there is any virtue and excellence, if there is anything worthy of praise, **I** think on, weigh, and take account of these things [fix **my** mind on them].

- *Philippians* 4:6-8

I seize, hold fast, and retain without wavering the hope **I** cherish and confess, for He Who promised is reliable and faithful to His word.

- *Hebrews* 10:23

I do not fling away **my** fearless confidence, for it carries a great and glorious compensation of reward.

- *Hebrews* 10:35

Now faith is the assurance (title deed, confirmation) of things I hope for (divinely guaranteed), and the evidence of things I can't see [the conviction of their reality—faith comprehends as fact what cannot be experienced by the physical senses].

- Hebrews 11:1

Jesus Christ (the Messiah) is [always] the same, yesterday, today, and forever (to the end of the age).

- Hebrews 13:8

If **I** am deficient in wisdom, **I** can ask of the giving God who gives to everyone liberally and ungrudgingly, without reproaching or faultfinding, and it will be given to **me**.

- James 1:5

I am subject to God. When **I** resist the devil and stand firm against him, he flees from **me**. As **I** come close to God, He comes close to **me**

- James 4:7

Am **I** sick? **I** should call on the church elders (the spiritual guides). And they should pray over **me**, anointing **me** with oil in the Lord's name. And the prayer of faith will save (heal, set free, deliver) **me**, and the Lord will restore **me**; and if **I** have committed sins, **I** will be forgiven.

- *James* 5:14-15

Jesus personally bore **my** sins in His own body on the tree as on an altar and offered Himself on it, that **I** might die to sin and live to righteousness. By His wounds and lashes **I** have been healed and made whole.

- 1 *Peter* 2:24

I cast the whole of **my** care [all **my** anxieties, all **my** worries, all **my** concerns, once and for all] on Jesus, for He cares for **me** affectionately and cares for **me** watchfully. **I** am well balanced (temperate, sober of mind), vigilant and cautious at all times; for **my** enemy, the devil, roams around like a lion roaring in fierce hunger, seeking someone to seize upon and devour. **I** withstand him and am firm in faith, knowing that the same (identical) sufferings are appointed to the whole body of Christians throughout the world.

- 1 Peter 5:7-9

If **my** conscience (**my** heart) does not accuse **me** [if it does not make **me** feel guilty and condemn **me**], **I** have confidence before God, And **I** receive from Him whatever **I** ask, because **I** [watchfully] obey God's orders [observe His suggestions and injunctions, follow His plan for **me**] and practice what is pleasing to Him.

- 1 John 3:21-22

And this is the confidence (the assurance, the privilege of boldness) which **I** have in the Lord: that if **I** ask anything (makes any request) according to His will (in agreement with His own plan), He listens to and hears **me**. And since **I** know that God listens to **me** in whatever **I** ask, **I** also know that **I** have the requests made of Him.

- 1 John 5:14-15

I prosper in every way and **my** body keeps well, even as **my** soul keeps well and prospers.

- 3 John 1:2

I have overcome (conquered) the enemy by means of the blood of the Lamb and by the speaking of **my** testimony...

- *Revelation* 12:11

A Prayer For Healing

If you are ready to receive healing today, or if you just want to release your faith for health and wholeness, you can receive right now. Jesus is your healer! You just read that throughout this whole book! Your part is to say and do. Say out loud, "Jesus is MY healer. He bore my sicknesses and my diseases and pain. I expect to receive now!"

Speak the following prayer in faith and mean it with your whole heart. Accept it and believe it!

Father, the Word of God that I have heard and confessed is the power of God unto salvation. I confess Jesus Christ as Lord over my life—spirit, soul and body. I receive the power of God to make me whole, sound, delivered, saved and healed now. I act on the Word of God and receive His power.

Sickness, disease and pain, I command you to go in the Name of Jesus. You are not the will of God for me. I enforce the Word of God on you. I will not tolerate you in my life. Leave my presence! I will never allow you back.

I have been healed and made sound. Jesus made me whole. My days of sickness and disease are over.

I am the saved. I am the healed. The power of sickness over my life has been broken forever. Jesus bore my sicknesses. Jesus bore my weakness. Jesus bore my pain—and I am free.

No sickness, sin, fear, or evil addiction shall lord over me any longer. I have been redeemed from the curse and I receive the blessing. I proclaim freedom in Jesus' Name. The gospel is the power of God to me unto salvation. I receive it. I act on it. I am made whole in the Name of the Lord Jesus Christ. Amen!

PRAYER FOR SALVATION AND BAPTISM IN THE HOLY SPIRIT

Heavenly Father, I come to You now in the Name of Jesus. Your Word says that, "Whosoever shall call on the name of the name of the Lord shall be saved" (Acts 2:21 KJV). I am calling on You. I pray and confess Jesus as Lord over my life according to Romans 10:9-10 (KJV): "If thou shalt confess with thy mouth the Lord Jesus, and shalt believe in thine heart that God hath raised him from the dead, thou shalt be saved. For with the heart man believeth unto righteousness; and with the mouth confession is made unto salvation." I do that now. I confess that Jesus is Lord, and I believe in my heart that God raised Him from the dead.

I am now reborn! I am a Christian—a child of Almighty God! I am saved!

You also said in your Word, "If ye then, being evil know how to give good gifts unto your children: HOW MUCH MORE shall your heavenly Father give the Holy Spirit to them that ask him?" (Luke 11:13 KJV). I'm asking now... fill me with your Holy Spirit. Holy Spirit, rise up within me as I praise God. I fully expect to speak with other tongues as you give me the utterance (Acts 2:4). In Jesus Name, Amen!

Begin to praise God for filling you with the Holy Spirit. Speak those words and syllables you receive—not in your own language, but the language given to you by the Holy Spirit. You have to use your own voice. God will not force you to speak. Don't be concerned with how it sounds. It is a heavenly language!

Praise God! You are a healed, born-again, Spirit-filled believer. You'll never be the same again. Find a good church that boldly preaches God's Word and obeys it. Become part of a church family who will love and care for you as you love and care for them.

MyVersion LLC.

We hope you enjoyed this healing scriptures book. Looking for an even more personalized experience? MyVersion Publishing offers this same book in nearly 100 popular male and female names.

You can find you or your friend's name on Amazon.com or on our website at MyVersionBook.com, these mini-books are a convenient 4x6 inch pocket sized paperback, ebook, audiobook, or Kindle; perfect for gift-giving or keeping in your pocket as a source of encouragement wherever you go.

We also have additional book series tailored to specific topics like peace from anxiety, finances, identity in Christ, and more; offering a personal touch that transforms scripture into a deeply meaningful experience.

By incorporating your name directly into the Scripture, MyVersion makes God's Word feel uniquely yours, helping you or your loved ones connect with faith on a whole new level.

Visit our website now to get your personalized books!

RICK'S

healing

SCRIPTURES

just for:
RICK

With long life will I satisfy **Rick** and show **him** My salvation.

- Psalm 91:16

Christ purchased **Rick's** freedom redeeming **him** from the curse of the Law and its condemnation by Himself becoming a curse for **Rick**, for it is written, cursed is everyone who hangs on a tree (is crucified);

- Galatians 3:13

Jesus personally bore **Rick's** sins in His own body on the tree as on an altar and offered Himself on it, that **Rick** might die to sin and live to righteousness. By His wounds and lashes **Rick** has been healed.

- 1 Peter 2:24